W9-BZH-484

Soaring

CARTER M. AYRES

Lerner Publications Company ■ Minneapolis, Minnesota

Fields Corner

ACKNOWLEDGMENTS: All photographs by the author except for the following: pp. 3, 26, 28, 39, George Uveges; pp. 4, 6, 14, 16, 18, 22, 36, Harris W. Holler. Cover photograph by George Uveges.

Acc. 11/87
870146 70-41

To Harris W. Holler

LIBRARY OF CONGRESS CATALOGING-IN-PUBLICATION DATA

Ayres, Carter M.
 Soaring.

 (Superwheels and thrill sports)
 Summary: An introduction to local and cross-country flight in gliders, including theories of weather, aerodynamics, and pilot technique.
 1. Gliding and soaring—Juvenile literature.
[1. Gliding] I. Title. II. Series: Superwheels & thrill sports.
J GV764.A97 1986 797.5'5 85-23667
ISBN 0-8225-0442-1 (lib. bdg.)

Manufactured in the United States of America

International Standard Book Number: 0-8225-0442-1
Library of Congress Catalog Number: 85-23667

 2 3 4 5 6 7 8 9 10 95 94 93 92 91 90 89 88 87

CONTENTS

INTRODUCTION

The feeling of flight is the reason people soar. It is a feeling that comes from flying with the wind, completely free of the earth, in a world of beauty and solitude. Unlike pilots of power planes who must rely on their engines to stay airborne, the pilot of a *sailplane*, or high-performance glider, becomes preoccupied with the forces of air at work in the sky. These natural forces become his or her engine.

To stay aloft, sailplane pilots must sense what is happening to the air that passes over the wings and tail of their aircraft. They must also learn to understand what is happening within the larger invisible sea of air in which they are flying. If they interpret this information correctly, it may be possible to soar for hours at a time.

Students at a German glider school in the 1930s. Gliding was a popular pastime in Germany during the years after World War I, and German pilots visiting the United States inspired American interest in the exciting sport.

SOARING'S BEGINNINGS

The history of soaring is full of fascinating stories about events that took place around the turn of the century. In their efforts to fly, people in the late 1800s jumped off cliffs, ran down hillsides, and were towed behind horse-drawn carriages. From their experimenting, a simple wing was developed that allowed a person, with legs dangling, to stay airborne for flights of up to 300 feet (90 meters).

Although the first full-sized glider was built in 1809, it was not until 1853 that a manned glider flight took place, and a glider that was controlled by the pilot was not flown until 1891. Prior to their first successful powered flight in 1903, the Wright brothers experimented with gliders and added a vertical fin, a horizontal stabilizer, and a body, or *fuselage*, to the wing.

Gliders developed at the same time as powered aircraft, and today's high-performance sailplanes are refinements of the gliders that were developed in Germany in the 1920s and 1930s. After German glider pilots visited Massachusetts in 1928, Americans became increasingly interested in sailplanes. The first gliders produced in the United States were built in 1930 in Elmira, New York, by the Schweizer brothers, and their company is still marketing many different models of sailplanes.

Today, with the encouragement and guidance of the Soaring Society of America (SSA), founded in 1932, soaring has become a highly developed sport in the United States. It is also popular in Canada, Australia, New Zealand, the U.S.S.R., and in many countries in South America and Europe.

A student prepares for takeoff under the watchful eye of soaring instructor Harris Holler. In the United States, soaring students may solo at age 14 and earn their private license by age 16.

THE SAILPLANE

WINGS

Sailplanes are designed with sleek, unbroken lines so they will stay in the air for as long as possible. The top of the wing is more curved than the bottom, and during flight air passes more quickly over the curved upper surface. This causes air pressure on top of the plane to become weaker and allows the wing to create *lift*—the upward force that opposes gravity—and to fly. By raising the sailplane's nose so the air pushes on the flat underside of the wing, the pilot gains additional lift for climbing, and the plane will rise even higher.

There will be problems, however, if the pilot raises the wing *too* high. As the wing moves up higher and higher, the air on top will no longer flow smoothly, and the increased air resistance, or *drag*, will cause the sailplane to slow down. When its speed decreases too much, the plane will stop flying and will *stall*, or lose lift, and begin to drop. To keep flying, the pilot must reduce the angle at which the wing strikes the air. A well-trained pilot can sense when a stall is coming and will lower the glider's nose before it happens.

CONTROL SURFACES

The cockpit is the sailplane's center of operations. Here the pilot sits and uses the *control stick* and *rudder pedals* to change the sailplane's direction, speed, and altitude.

7

The cockpit of a high-performance sailplane. In the foreground of the photograph is the control stick, which is strapped down with the seat belt to prevent the wind from moving wing and tail surfaces while the aircraft is on the ground. The rudder pedals are forward of the control panel, in the plane's nose.

When the control stick is moved sideways, the glider's *ailerons* (the movable panels at the *trailing*, or rear, edge of each wing tip) will roll the wing to the right or to the left. When the control stick is moved forward or backward, the *elevator* (the hinged horizontal surface on the glider's tail) pitches the nose up or down. When the rudder pedals are moved with the feet, the rudder *yaws*, or rotates, the nose to the right and to the left.

All sailplanes have two other control surfaces. The *spoilers* are narrow plates, or slats, embedded in each wing. When the pilot is ready to descend and approach the runway, he or she raises the spoilers, or "air brakes," by pulling back on a lever in the cockpit. This creates extra drag by disturbing the air flowing across the top of the wings.

In this photo of a sailplane's wing, you can see the curved upper surface that generates lift for flying. Also visible is the spoiler *(top)* and the wing flap *(foreground)*. The aileron is located next to the wing's tip.

Preflight check completed, a sailplane pilot relaxes in the sun while waiting for his towplane *(right)* to taxi into position for takeoff.

SOARING

PREFLIGHT CHECKS

Before every flight, the pilot conducts a preflight check of the sailplane to make sure that it is *airworthy*, or ready to fly. This check is particularly important if others have handled or flown the sailplane or if it has not been flown recently. During the preflight check, everything from the cable release mechanism on the nose to the elevator on the tail will be examined to see that it is in working order. The following specific checks must be made: **The Pitot Tube.** This device, which measures how fast the sailplane is moving forward, should be free from dirt and insects. The sailplane's *airspeed indicator* records its speed in miles per hour.

Control Surface Connections. All connections such as hinges, cables, nuts, and bolts should be checked to see that they have been properly assembled and tightened and are not worn. **Wings and Tail Assembly.** Special attention should be given to the condition of the wing tips. The wing tips are more likely to be damaged than other parts of the glider because they are so exposed. **Static Ports.** These openings in the fuselage, which help to run the *altimeter*, must also be free from dirt and any other obstructions. When the sailplane climbs higher or descends, the altimeter reads the atmospheric pressure from the static ports and shows the sailplane's altitude in feet above sea level. **Canopy.** This transparent enclosure over the cockpit must be very clean and highly polished. Good visibility is essential for sailplane pilots to see other aircraft, to search for lift, and to monitor their *track* (the ground path over which the sailplane flies). Clear visibility also makes the flight more enjoyable.

After completing the external check of the sailplane, the pilot enters the cockpit to check the functioning of the following instruments and controls:

Altimeter. The altimeter, which indicates altitude, should be adjusted to show the elevation of the airport above sea level.

Seat Belt and Shoulder Straps. These straps must be securely and comfortably fastened. If used properly, they will prevent injuries to the head when flying in turbulent weather.

Control Stick. The control stick must operate smoothly, and the pilot must be able to move it freely in all directions. This is essential for safe operation while in the air, especially during takeoffs and landings.

Spoilers and Flaps. The spoilers must be closed, and the *flaps* (additional hinged panels between the ailerons and fuselage), if any, set for takeoff to give the plane maximum lift while being towed for takeoff.

Cable and Cable Release. The *cable*, or towline, must be securely fastened to the nose of the sailplane, and the *cable release* should function smoothly. This check is done with the help of a *wingman*, a person standing on the ground alongside the aircraft.

Canopy. The canopy must be securely closed and locked to prevent it from flying open during takeoff.

Testing the cable release mechanism is an important part of the preflight check. This photo shows a pilot opening and closing the cable release in response to the wingman's hand signals.

"Let's roll!" A wingman makes a circular movement with his arm to let the towplane pilot know that the sailplane is ready for takeoff.

AEROTOW

When the pilot is sure that the sailplane will work properly once its in the air, or *airborne*, a "thumbs up" sign to the wingman signals that the plane is ready for launching. At the sign, the wingman will lift the wing of the sailplane that has been on the ground so that both wings are level. Now the pilot must make a final decision about whether or not to take off. If "yes," he or she will waggle the rudder back and forth to signal the towplane pilot—who has already taken up the slack in the connecting cable—to begin the takeoff. The wingman confirms this by moving one arm around in a circle. There is nothing left to do but to fly!

While being towed to the proper altitude, the sailplane pilot must keep the towplane centered in the windshield and must make all turns *with* the towplane, staying either below or above the *wash*, or air disturbance, that is created by the towplane's propellor. All turns should be made cleanly so that there will be no increase in drag from sloppy flying. Because drag will cause a sailplane to lose altitude more quickly, precise flying skills could make the difference between having enough altitude to make it back to the airport or having to land short in a farmer's field—or worse!

An experienced sailplane pilot can learn to estimate airspeed by listening to the sound of the air rushing past the plane.

AIRSPEED

To have a safe and enjoyable flight, the pilot must know how to choose and maintain an appropriate airspeed. For example, when circling in a *thermal* (a rising body of warm air) to gain altitude, it is important to fly at *minimum sink speed,* which is about seven miles an hour (11km/h) above *stall speed* (the speed at which the wing can no longer hold an aircraft's altitude). But when flying cross-country, the pilot must fly more quickly between thermals so that as little altitude as possible will be lost.

Although a pilot can check on the airspeed by looking at the airspeed indicator from time to time, a better way to check is to learn how to determine speed by the sound and the feel of the sailplane itself. For example, when flying very slowly, the pilot won't hear much noise from the air passing over the plane, and the control stick will feel as though it has little effect on the position, or *attitude,* of the aircraft. Such clues will alert a knowledgable pilot to an approaching stall, a condition that could prove to be dangerous.

If the plane is about to stall, the pilot's first move must be to gain speed and reduce drag. This is done by lowering the nose and by lowering the spoilers, if they have been raised. If the sailplane is turning, the pilot will also level the wings. Turns increase a sailplane's stall speed; in fact, a sailplane that stalls during a turn may enter a *spin.*

Spins are more dangerous than stalls because it takes longer for a sailplane to regain its ability to fly after a spin. In a spin, the sailplane will descend in a steep spiraling turn with at least one of its wings stalled. While spinning earthward, the sailplane may fall 1,000 feet (300m) or more before the pilot is able to "pull out" of the spin. For this reason, a stall at low-altitude spin can lead to a very serious accident.

A sailplane banks into a turn. The sleek aircraft shown here is a Schweizer SGU 1-20, a modification of one of the early gliders built by the Schweizer brothers in 1946.

TURNS

To fly cleanly—precisely and efficiently—through a turn, a pilot must use the control stick and the rudder pedals at the same time. When the pilot *banks* (inclines to one side) the wing by moving the stick sideways, some of the wing's lift is used up by pulling the sailplane and its occupant around to a new *heading*, or direction. To prevent the sailplane from sinking, the pilot also pulls back on the stick, which creates more lift. At the same time, he or she operates the rudder pedals to help push the nose into and through the turn. By coordinating stick and rudder, the pilot can guide the plane through a precise and controlled turn.

While steering the glider with both hands and feet, the pilot must be careful not to lose too much altitude during turns. The pilot can check on the altitude by keeping an eye on a *yaw string*, which is often just a 3-inch (7.5-centimeter) piece of yarn taped to the center line of the *canopy*, or top, of the cockpit. If the yaw string streams straight back rather than to left or right, the craft is flying smoothly through the air in a low-drag turn, and it is neither *slipping*—from using too little rudder—or *skidding*—from using too much rudder. Slips and skids create drag, decreasing the sailplane's ability to stay aloft.

Coming in for a landing, the pilot eases back on the control stick until the sailplane stalls, sinks down, and makes contact with the ground.

FINAL APPROACH AND LANDING

Flying well will also pay off in the *traffic pattern*—the aerial course around the runway that leads to the desired touchdown point— when the pilot is making the landing approach. During the traffic pattern, the pilot must maintain a constant *pattern airspeed*—a speed of 1.5 times the sailplane's stall speed plus the wind velocity. Using pattern airspeed avoids stalls and spins while making the necessary turns toward the runway. Throughout the approach, the pilot monitors the track over the ground. Checking the track will tell the pilot what effect the wind is having on the sailplane and what adjustments in the heading must be made so that he or she will touch down safely.

During the final stages of approach, the pilot descends to just one or two feet (30-60cm) over the runway. At this point, the speed is reduced more and more by easing back on the control stick. As drag increases and airspeed drops off, the sailplane sinks, stalls, and gently touches down. Landing is one time when a stall is helpful in controlling the sailplane.

When being towed, a sailplane must be kept in proper alignment with the towplane. This Schleicher K-8 sailplane is being towed over the beautiful Cannon River Valley in Minnesota.

IN THE AIR

Although learning how to land properly is important, sailplane pilots spend most of their time—both on the ground and in the air—looking for ways to stay *up* instead of coming down! In still air, the force of gravity causes a sailplane to descend gently to earth at about 200 feet (60m) per minute. Therefore, if the pilot were released from the towline at 1,000 feet (300m), his or her flight would last only five minutes.

To offset the sailplane's natural earthward movement, the pilot looks for *rising air.* As long as the speed of the rising air is faster than the sailplane's rate of descent, the pilot has the *possibility* of staying airborne indefinitely. When the pilot finds rising air and glides within it so that it carries the craft aloft, he or she is no longer gliding—but *soaring!*

To find lift for soaring, the pilot must use visible clues and his or her own "sky sense." For example, while scanning the world below, the pilot will keep a sharp lookout for circling birds, smoke rising from a bonfire or a smokestack, *cumulus clouds* (clouds with a flat base and rounded top and sides)—and even other sailplanes. The feel of the wings rocking gently up and down will tell the pilot that the glider has flown into something good—air going *up*!

THERMALING

The word pilots use for rising air is *thermal*. Thermals are the upward winds created when air, heated by the ground, rises upward—like hot air balloons. As they ascend, thermals move across the sky with the wind.

Thermals gradually cool as they continue to rise, and their moisture condenses and becomes visible, creating clouds. Eventually, the entire bubble of air will cool and stop rising. At this point, the cloud will *decay*, or break up, and disappear.

Sailplane pilots looking for thermals always look for clouds, especially clouds with clearly defined edges. Such edges mean the cloud is not yet complete and a thermal is still rising below it. A *concave* (inwardly rounded) base also indicates that air is rising and entering under the cloud. Pilots avoid clouds with ragged edges, for these signal cloud decay and the end of thermal activity.

When the air is full of thermals and their cumulus clouds, the sailplane pilot may be able to stay aloft simply by flying straight from one thermal to the next. When relatively few thermals exist, however, the pilot has to begin *thermaling*, or turning in tight circles, to stay within the rising air.

As a pilot flies into a thermal, he or she can find out the rate of ascent in feet per minute by looking at the *variometer* on the instrument panel. When gliding from one thermal to another, the variometer will indicate how much altitude the plane is losing per minute.

Thermaling requires the same kind of precise flying that is needed for turning in a traffic pattern. To reduce drag and gain the most altitude, a pilot should fly at minimum sink airspeed and as precisely as possible. The pilot must also be aware of the direction of the wind so that he or she can stay within the thermal as it drifts across the countryside.

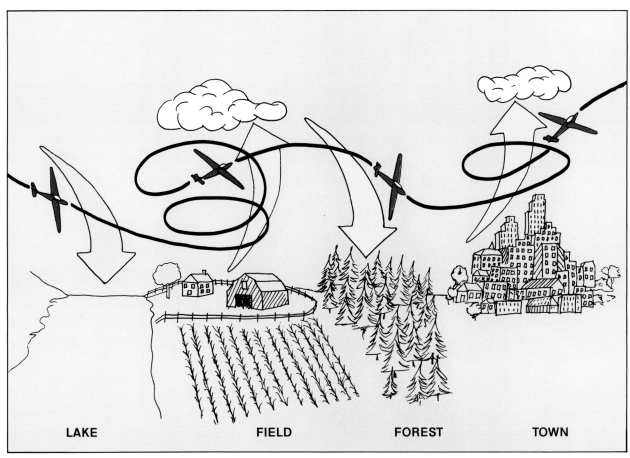

LAKE   FIELD   FOREST   TOWN

Thermals are created by air warmed through contact with heated areas of the ground. Dry, flat surfaces such as roads, plowed fields, and buildings absorb heat from the sun and warm the air above them. Cool surfaces like lakes, on the other hand, cool the air, creating downdrafts. To stay aloft, a sailplane pilot must move from thermal to thermal. Sometimes it is necessary to turn the plane in tight circles in order to stay within a column of rising air.

The pilot of a Schreder HP-11 rides the rising air sweeping up a mountain ridge.

RIDGE SOARING

Pilots can also find rising air by flying close to a mountain ridge. A *ridge* is a long and narrow range of hills or mountains that may stretch for miles. Air rises along a ridge when the wind approaches it from one side, and usually there will be enough lift for soaring when there is a wind speed of 10 to 20 miles per hour (16-32 km/h) and the mountains are at least 800 feet (240m) high. Unlike thermals, which can take a sailplane up 15,000 feet (4,500m) or higher, a pilot soaring in ridge lift can only fly about 100 to 200 feet (30-60m) above the ridge.

Ridge lift is safe to fly as long as the pilot does not stray across to the ridge's *lee*, or downwind, side. As the air rises over the ridge, it tumbles down the lee side, creating both sink and *turbulence*. To avoid this bumpy, swirling, descending air, the pilot should only fly along the ridge's upwind side.

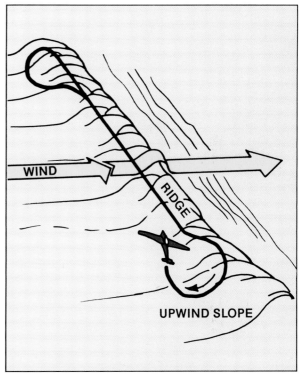

WIND

RIDGE

UPWIND SLOPE

Air rising over a mountain ridge creates lift for a sailplane flying along the upwind slope.

Mountain ridges also produce columns of rising air called waves, which can lift sailplanes to great altitudes.

WAVE SOARING

A third source of rising air is called a *wave*. Waves form on the downwind side of mountain ridges as the air spilling over the ridge drops down, hits the valley floor, becomes compressed, and then bounces back up to a tremendous height. Acting much like a rubber ball, a wave bounces up and down on its way across the countryside. If a pilot releases from the towplane far enough downwind of a ridge or mountain range, he or she may encounter the enormous power of a rising wave.

Waves create strong lift that allows soaring pilots—if they are wearing heavy clothes and are equipped with oxygen—to make high-altitude climbs in excess of 30,000 feet (9,000m) and cross-country flights of several hundred miles. To do this, they must stay near the upwind edge of the wave, because to penetrate too far downwind is highly dangerous. The mass of turbulent air, called a *rotor*, located at the wave's center can be strong enough to tear off the wings of even high-performance sail planes built to stand up to great stress.

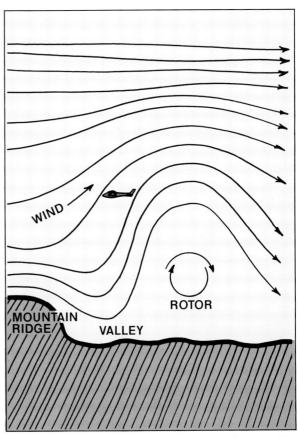

Waves are formed on the downwind side of mountains when air bounces up after crossing a ridge and sinking down to the valley floor. In riding a wave, a sailplane pilot must be sure to avoid the dangerous rotor of turbulent air at its center.

Once a pilot has mastered practice flights within gliding range of an airport, the next step is taking a short cross-country flight.

CROSS-COUNTRY SOARING

Beginning pilots usually practice near their local airports, knowing that they can always glide back home and land safely on familiar terrain. They quickly learn where the best lift can be found and what local wind and weather conditions are like during the year.

As pilots become more experienced, however, they will want to test their soaring skills in a new and more challenging environment— the sky away from home. While flying cross-country, a pilot's thinking, knowledge, and instincts will be tested many times as he or she works to stay aloft over a course that may be as far as 300 miles (480km) away.

A pilot's first cross-country flight will usually be a relatively short excursion of about 30 miles (48km). As one experienced instructor has put it, a first cross-country flight is just a matter of "tossing the pilot out of the nest." On a good soaring day—when the wind is about 10 miles an hour (16km/h) and the "cu's" (cumulus clouds) are starting to form— the pilot tows out, catches a thermal, and releases. He or she works the sailplane up to the base of the cloud above and then floats downwind. After circling for a few minutes, the pilot looks below and sees a small airport and a crew waiting to trailer him or her back home. This success encourages the pilot to attempt a longer trip next time.

Long-distance soaring provides the ultimate test of a pilot's knowledge and skill.

LONG-DISTANCE CROSS-COUNTRY SOARING

Long-distance cross-country soaring requires more planning and preparation than shorter trips. The self-confidence that is necessary for a successful flight comes from knowing when and where lift may be found and how to use it effectively. Being a good cross-country pilot is hard work, and it requires a combination of self-discipline, judgment, and practiced "stick 'n rudder" skill.

Before the flight, the pilot may have to first fly the course in a power plane or drive along it in a car. This excursion will familiarize the pilot with the lay of the land so that thermals, ridge lift, and waves may be more easily found.

The pilot will also study an aeronautical chart of the area around the proposed course so that landmarks can be identified from the air. Symbols on the chart will indicate roads, lakes, small towns, water towers, railroads, and gravel pits. Studying these ahead of time will help the pilot keep track of his or her progress and position during the flight.

Before a cross-country flight, the pilot should check weather reports several times a day to become aware of current weather developments. With this knowledge, the pilot will be better able to anticipate what weather changes may occur in the immediate future. The longer the flight, the more the pilot will need to have up-to-date information about weather conditions.

The instruments on a sailplane's control panel provide important information about the flight. The aircraft's speed is shown by the airspeed indicator *(upper left)*, while the variometer *(right)* tells the pilot how fast the plane is sinking or rising. A magnetic compass also helps the pilot to keep his or her bearings while gliding from one source of lift to another.

From time to time—usually for lack of enough lift—it will be necessary for even the best pilot to simply call it quits and land short of his or her goal. But even a shortened trip can be exhilarating. Part of the joy of soaring over a long distance is experienced *after* touchdown when one can relax and share every detail of the flight with other pilots and crew members.

While cross-country flying offers increased challenges, risks increase *only* when pilots use poor judgment instead of common sense. Unfortunately, some people falsely believe that being a good pilot means taking unnecessary risks. Others exceed the limits of their knowledge and flying experience and attempt flights for which they do not have the proper training. Those who plan ahead and realize the consequences of their actions, however, will be safe and capable sailplane pilots.

As this plane turns toward the runway during final approach, its pilot continually monitors the aircraft's condition by visual observation and by the "feel" of the controls.

Sailplane pilots prepare for a regional soaring competition in Minnesota during the early 1970s.

COMPETITION FLYING

The Soaring Sociey of America (SSA) awards silver, gold, and diamond badges for a variety of soaring achievements. The silver badge requirements include flying a distance of 50 kilometers (about 30 miles) and an altitude gain of 1,000 meters (about 3,300 feet). The gold and diamond requirements are more challenging, and the diamond badge includes a distance flight of 500 kilometers (300 miles) and an altitude gain of 5,000 meters (16,500 feet, or about 3 miles).

Although not all of the requirements have to be accomplished during the same flight, each must be confirmed by an officially designated SSA observer. In addition, photographs and *barograph* tracings taken in the sailplane en route that show the altitude and the time must be furnished.

A sailplane crew makes last-minute preparations for a world championship soaring competition. Prize-winning pilots from all over the world participate in this event, which is held every two years.

Each year, the SSA also sponsors a number of contests at soaring centers throughout the United States. Here, pilots at all levels of experience participate in competition at local, regional, and national levels.

Regional and national contests are designated by the kind of sailplanes that compete. *Unlimited class* sailplanes are the highest performance gliders. Their wingspans stretch 22 meters (about 72 feet) from tip to tip, and they may glide more than 40 feet forward for every foot they descend. *Fifteen-meter-class* sailplanes have somewhat shorter wingspans, and they are only slightly lower in performance. *Standard-class* sailplanes also have wingspans of 15 meters (about 50 feet), but they have no wing flaps. Finally, a "one-design" class of sailplanes used in competition is the *Schweizer 1-26*. After preliminary training, many new soaring pilots graduate to the 1-26 and use it in competition flying.

Pilots who perform well at the local and regional levels qualify for competition in the nationals. No matter what kind of sailplane they fly, these pilots fly for speed around a triangular course that may be from 100 to 300 kilometers (60 to 180 miles) in length. Competing pilots must use all of their cross-country knowledge and ingenuity to make it around the course—and to do it faster than anyone else.

CONCLUSION

Sailplane pilots know that they must develop excellent flying skills because *they*, and not an engine, must keep their craft airborne. They also know that knowledge, planning, and practice will allow them to experience a unique relationship with the wind and the sky. As they circle in silence for hours at a time, they will know the sense of freedom, accomplishment, and quiet joy that comes from flying the wind.

Airplanes
  AEROBATICS
  AIRPLANE RACING
  FLYING-MODEL AIRPLANES
  HELICOPTERS
  HOME-BUILT AIRPLANES
  PERSONAL AIRPLANES
  RECORD-BREAKING AIRPLANES
  SCALE-MODEL AIRPLANES
  YESTERDAY'S AIRPLANES
  UNUSUAL AIRPLANES

Automobiles & Auto Racing
  AMERICAN RACE CAR DRIVERS
  THE DAYTONA 500
  DRAG RACING
  ICE RACING
  THE INDIANAPOLIS 500
  INTERNATIONAL RACE CAR DRIVERS
  LAND SPEED RECORD BREAKERS
  RACING YESTERDAY'S CARS
  RALLYING
  ROAD RACING
  TRACK RACING

  CLASSIC SPORTS CARS
  CUSTOM CARS
  DINOSAUR CARS: LATE GREAT CARS
    FROM 1945 TO 1966

FABULOUS CARS OF THE 1920s & 1930s
KIT CARS: CARS YOU CAN BUILD YOURSELF
MODEL CARS
RESTORING YESTERDAY'S CARS
VANS: THE PERSONALITY VEHICLES
YESTERDAY'S CARS

Bicycles
  BICYCLE MOTOCROSS RACING
  BICYCLE ROAD RACING
  BICYCLE TRACK RACING
  BICYCLES ON PARADE

Motorcycles
  GRAND NATIONAL CHAMPIONSHIP RACES
  MOPEDS: THE GO-EVERYWHERE BIKES
  MOTOCROSS MOTORCYCLE RACING
  MOTORCYCLE RACING
  MOTORCYCLES ON THE MOVE
  THE WORLD'S BIGGEST MOTORCYCLE RACE:
    THE DAYTONA 200

Other Specialties
  BALLOONING
  KARTING
  MOUNTAIN CLIMBING
  RIVER THRILL SPORTS
  SAILBOAT RACING
  SOARING
  SPORT DIVING
  SKYDIVING
  SNOWMOBILE RACING
  YESTERDAY'S FIRE ENGINES
  YESTERDAY'S TRAINS
  YESTERDAY'S TRUCKS

Lerner Publications Company
241 First Avenue North, Minneapolis, Minnesota 55401